What people are saying about

Pagan Portals – Guided Visualisations

Guided visualisations are a c̲̅ spi ̲ʾuse you can have an adventure wit̲ʰ ʾr, journeys of the imagination ̲ ̲ero carbon-footprint! This book i̲s̲ ̲tions and activities for all seasons. It range ̲things being revealed on a beach to planting seec ̲ove. The technique can be used for problem-solving, visioning and managing anxiety (the possibilities are limitless). Put yourself in the safe hands of a modern pagan witch and fasten your "psychic seatbelt!"
Imelda Almqvist, international teacher and author of three books including *Natural Born Shamans: A Spiritual Toolkit for Life* and *Sacred Art: A Hollow Bone for Spirit*

Guided visualisations are always magical in that they can take you on journeys into your subconscious to reveal hidden secrets, information or insights that can serve you well and have practical applications in your life. It is so useful to have a whole range of them, of varying lengths and purposes, to dip in and out of as the mood or need takes. Although written by a 'modern pagan witch' these guided visualisations are easy to access by anyone of any background or belief system. This is a great resource for anyone to have in their bag or on their bookshelf and for teachers or trainers it will provide a useful tool to use with students.
Yvonne Reeves, author of *Shaman Pathways – Web of Life*, Reiki Master and Shamanic Healer

Lucya's book is a thorough and extremely engaging exploration of guided visualisation, full of beautifully written and carefully thought out ready-to-use visualisations appropriate for people of all abilities. One of my favourite things about this book is the many different ways these visualisations explore the imagery of nature. Themes of love, discovery, the wheel of the year and elemental power mean everyone should be able to find something that resonates with them. I would recommend this book to anyone who has an interest in exploring the powers of the mind, both conscious and subconscious, and for anyone who enjoys using their imagination. This is a book I will return to again and again and will use with my own students to aid them in their own visualisation experiences.

Mabh Savage, author of *A Modern Celt, Seeking the Ancestors* and *Pagan Portals: Celtic Witchcraft*

Pagan Portals
Guided Visualisations

Pathways into Wisdom and Witchcraft

Pagan Portals

Guided Visualisations

Pathways into Wisdom and Witchcraft

Lucya Starza

MOON
BOOKS

Winchester, UK
Washington, USA

JOHN HUNT PUBLISHING

First published by Moon Books, 2020
Moon Books is an imprint of John Hunt Publishing Ltd., No. 3 East Street, Alresford
Hampshire SO24 9EE, UK
office@jhpbooks.net
www.johnhuntpublishing.com
www.moon-books.net

For distributor details and how to order please visit the 'Ordering' section on our website.

Text copyright: Lucya Starza 2019

ISBN: 978 1 78904 567 3
978 1 78904 568 0 (ebook)
Library of Congress Control Number: 2019956894

A CIP catalogue record for this book is available from the British Library.

Design: Stuart Davies

UK: Printed and bound by CPI Group (UK) Ltd, Croydon, CR0 4YY
US: Printed and bound by Thomson-Shore, 7300 West Joy Road, Dexter, MI 48130

We operate a distinctive and ethical publishing philosophy in
all areas of our business, from our global network of authors to
production and worldwide distribution.

Contents

Other Titles by Lucya Starza

Candle Magic
A witch's guide to spells and rituals
978-1-78535-043-6 (paperback)
978-1-78535-044-3 (e-book)

Poppets and Magical Dolls
Dolls for spellwork, witchcraft and seasonal celebrations
978-1-78535-721-3 (paperback)
978-1-78535-722-0 (e-book)

Introduction

The Start of the Journey

Let me guide you to amazing places. It will be an adventure, I promise you. There are discoveries to make, secrets to learn and mysteries to unravel. They are your own secrets and mysteries, but no one will pry into them except yourself. I will lead you – at least at first – but you will learn to find your own way too. I will show you how to stay safe on your travels and teach you to plot your own pathways into wisdom and witchcraft.

The journeys in this book are all ones using the mind – guided visualisations of doorways to go through, paths to follow, places to explore and encounters to be experienced.

Learning the Language

I have called this book *Pagan Portals – Guided Visualisations*. You might have heard the terms 'guided meditation', 'guided visualisation', 'creative visualisation', 'pathworking' and 'journeying' used for experiences using the mind's eye. They are related and often similar, but have slight differences in meaning. Their purposes and the history of how they developed are also different.

Meditation

Meditation involves techniques to help you concentrate your attention. Some forms involve mindfulness and often have the aim of helping the practitioner remain in the moment, observing but not engaging any thinking processes. They can involve focussing on breathing in and out, or on other physical actions or parts of the body. They can also be done by observing patterns such as mandalas or natural phenomena. A guided meditation can include visualising an image in the mind to focus on, and can be very much like a guided visualisation – the definitions aren't always completely separate. Other forms of meditation are intended to help practitioners transcend conscious thought completely and are generally associated with religious traditions that see transcending as a spiritual goal.

The techniques of meditation originate in Buddhism and Taoism, although they can be similar to some passive contemplations in other spiritual paths, including Christian and pagan contemplative practices. These days, mindfulness is often used in a non-spiritual way, purely for relaxation and mental wellbeing. Meditation can be a good thing to do before attempting a guided visualisation because it helps you get into a relaxed state and a frame of mind where you are focussing your concentration.

Guided Visualisation and Creative Visualisation

Although some meditation techniques use simple visualisations, in general guided visualisation is different from meditation because the symbolic or archetypal qualities of what is visualised are often more important than stilling the mind. As Yvonne Aburrow writes in her book *Dark Mirror: The Inner Work of Witchcraft*:

> A visualisation invites you to focus on specific images; sometimes it tells a story or involves travelling through a landscape (real or imaginary);... Visualisation is a journey of the imagination (though not necessarily an imaginary journey).'

The difference between a guided visualisation and a creative visualisation is that the latter is specifically intended to help you manifest a goal; and can be used as part of casting a spell. Guided visualisation is more about developing intuition and learning to better understand oneself, the world, and unseen forces. Guided visualisations, and the psychic journeys and experiences I describe in this book, are in some ways similar to intuitive scrying or divination, but using a story to aid the process rather than, say, oracle or tarot cards.

As well as being designed to help you know yourself better, the guided visualisations in this book can help you find potential solutions to problems, get ideas for creative and artistic projects, see possible ways forward in life, attune yourself to the cycles of nature, and increase wisdom in general. They can also be used as a wellbeing tool, reducing stress and anxiety through relaxation techniques as well as by improving self-knowledge and confidence.

Many guided visualisations have spiritual aspects, but are not exclusive to any one tradition. I am a modern pagan witch, and I devised many of the following visualisations to help trainee witches improve their own understanding of the elements, the Wheel of the Year and the power of the Moon, and by that develop the necessary symbolic and personal knowledge. There is one creative visualisation in this book, for Yuletide wishes, which goes beyond guided visualisation and into spellwork. There is an overlap between guided visualisation and creative visualisation, as this shows.

Pathworking

The term pathworking historically comes from the Kabbala, although the techniques used are essentially guided visualisations. The Kabbalistic Tree of Life is depicted as having 22 paths connecting spheres that are the domains of ten Sephiroth, or attributes of the divine. By visualising movement along these paths, practitioners encounter specific symbols that help them learn the lessons necessary for progress within the Kabbalistic system. The landscapes, beings and objects encountered in pathworkings are specific to Kabbalistic work, and also correspond to the cards of the major arcana in tarot.

Although many of the guided visualisations in this book do involve travelling along paths, they are pagan paths, not the paths of the Tree of Life. I prefer not to use the term pathworking because of its specific meaning.

Journeying

Journeying is a term used in shamanic practices and often means travelling to other realms or alternative realities in a spiritual capacity. It often involves going into a trance using drumming or other rhythmic sounds, or by the use of entheogenic plants. This book is not about shamanic journeying in that sense, and does not cover those techniques. However, it can be useful to try out guided visualisations before going on to learn shamanic journeying.

Trancework and other forms of hypnosis take you much deeper into your subconscious than guided visualisations are intended to. Although guided visualisations do require you to be relaxed and enable you to engage with images and symbols that might arise from the subconscious, what you are primarily doing is using your imagination and intuition. You should still be conscious of your mind working, and have a general sense of connection to your body, while you are doing visualisations. I don't want anyone reading this book to get lost in some other reality or plane of existence!

Personal Work

While it is useful to understand that the terms meditation, visualisation, pathworking and journeying all have different origins and histories, I don't think you need to be too purist in your own personal work. There's a lot of interplay and similarity between the techniques and purposes of guided meditations, visualisations and pathworkings. It's okay to use the term you feel comfortable with.

Are you Sitting Comfortably?

When you are doing a guided visualisation, it is very important that you are in a safe place where you will not be disturbed, because you will be there for some time with your eyes closed. Your own living room is often ideal. Ensure that you are going to be comfortable for the entire duration. Ideally, you should be seated, with your back supported, but if you are unable to sit then you can do the visualisation lying down. Do make sure you are not going to fall asleep or fall over. It is particularly important that you never do a guided visualisation while operating machinery or driving. Get the temperature right. If you think you might get cold, wrap yourself in a blanket or put on an extra layer of clothing.

Those are all important parts of physical safety. Mental safety is important too. Ideally, read any guided visualisation before doing it. There is a big difference between simply reading something and immersing yourself in it to interact with the narrative it in a psychic way. If you feel it touches on areas you do not wish to contemplate, then do not attempt it. If you feel you need to stop a guided visualisation before the end, you can. Mentally tell yourself that you are stopping the visualisation and returning in your mind to a safe place. Then, concentrate on the physical sense of your body. Be aware of your breathing, wiggle your toes and fingers, feel the floor or earth beneath your feet, then slowly open your eyes.

After you have finished, it is important to ground properly. This can best be done by having something to eat and a non-alcoholic drink, but you can also stamp your feet on the floor a few times to feel its solidity, or grip a solid surface, such as the edge of a table, to feel a physical connection with reality.

Note: The guided visualisations in this book are intended for those of an adult age. Guided visualisations should not be done by anyone who is suffering from mental illness, except by the approval of a suitably qualified mental health professional.

How to do Guided Visualisations

Ideally, guided visualisations are best done with the eyes closed. In a practical sense, if you are on your own, that means recording each visualisation before you do it for real. You could use your phone or your laptop to record it. Play it back to yourself, pausing when necessary in order to fully visualise each part. If you are part of a group, one person can read the text while the others have their eyes closed. If neither of those methods are possible for you, then read to yourself as you go, closing your eyes after each short passage to do the visualisation, then opening your eyes to do the next bit, then closing them again, and so on.

Read each sentence slowly, then allow sufficiently long gaps between passages in which to concentrate on what was described or asked within it. In your mind's eye, try to see, hear, smell or otherwise experience the scene and any activities taking place within it. Many people will visualise those things as pictures or movie-like images in their imagination, but some get sounds or scents more readily than pictures. That is fine. Others will feel a connection with the words that tell the story, but see few or no images. That is also okay. Do what is right for you personally. If you are using a recording, have your finger on the pause button in case you need a longer pause than you originally anticipated to visualise each scene.

Sometimes you will find that your mind takes you in a different direction to the narrative. It is up to you to decide whether you want to gently draw your attention back to the guided passages or see where your own mind is taking you; although if you are a beginner, I would recommend trying to stick to the script if you can. When you are more experienced you can be more adventurous.

It can be useful to take notes after finishing a guided visualisation, but don't do them during it, as that will break your immersion in what is happening. Like a dream, the events that take place in a visualisation can fade from memory in time. If you want to recall it later, having notes can be helpful. Sometimes the meanings of things you saw or that happened will become more apparent later on. If you prefer not to write notes, you can record your thoughts on the same device as the visualisation; you could make a drawing of what you saw – or even write a poem about it. If you are in a group doing the same visualisation at the same time, afterwards, you can share your experiences and any insights gained. Or you can just enjoy the memories if that is what feels right to you. It is always your choice.

About the Guided Visualisations in this Book

Many books on guided visualisations are written from a mind, body, spirit perspective. I am a modern pagan witch and have been for decades. I developed much of the material in this book for use by trainee witches and for those on similar earth-based spiritual paths following the Wheel of the Year festivals.

The first chapter covers short visualisations to introduce the techniques. These guided visualisations are not specifically pagan or witchy, but are intended as aids to self-knowledge and wisdom. The next chapter is a series of visualisations on the pagan Wheel of the Year that can be used as part of seasonal rites. Many witches meet every month at the time of the full moon, as that is when magic works best, so I have included a ritual on the power of the moon after the visualisations for the year's solar cycle. This is followed by visualisations on the elements earth, air, fire, and water. Trainee witches are often required to study the elements as a good way of understanding them as they are important symbols and correspondences required for spellwork. Then there are three visualisations to help you develop psychic powers and assist with creative or artistic inspiration and ideas. Finally, there is a chapter on how to write guided visualisations.

I recommend doing the first one in the book before any others, as it is designed to help you create a safe place to return to in your mind if you need to during other visualisations.

So, if you are sitting comfortably, let's begin...

Chapter 1

Short Guided Visualisations

Guided visualisations don't have to be long to be effective. If you are new to the technique, I would recommend starting out with a short, simple one, ideally the first one in this section. It is called Your Safe Place and is designed to help you create a strong image of somewhere safe that you can return to any time you like if you are doing another visualisation, but want it to end early. It provides a symbolic key you can visualise to immediately transport you in your mind's eye to your safe place.

Your Safe Place

Find somewhere to sit safely in a place where you will not be disturbed. Ensure that you are warm and comfortable. Close your eyes. Relax your body. Take a deep breath in, hold it for a moment, let the breath go fully out. Pause for a moment, then take another deep breath in. Hold it for a moment, let it go out. Do that one more time. Now you are ready to start the guided visualisation.

With your eyes still closed, in your mind's eye, imagine the safest, most comfortable, most beautiful, happiest place you can think of. It might be somewhere that really exists, somewhere you remember from the past, somewhere you have seen in a picture, or somewhere completely imaginary. Spend some time visualising the place in your mind's eye.

Perhaps you can see it clearly as a mental picture, but not everyone visualises things in that way. Perhaps you only see the important aspects of the space – that's fine. Perhaps you find it easier to describe it to yourself with words in your head. That's also fine. Perhaps you find it easier to imagine what it is like to touch the objects around you, the surface beneath you, the feel of the movement of air on your skin. Perhaps it is the sounds of this place, or the scents that are most vivid to you. Perhaps you get a mixture of all of those things. These ways of visualising are all fine. This is your space; this is your visualisation.

Spend a little time experiencing these things in your mind. Enjoy them. Stay here for as long as you need to familiarise yourself with this space.

After a while you notice a small, lightweight item somewhere in this safe and lovely space. You know that this item has magical properties. It is a kind of key that will always return you to this safe space if you need to when on guided visualisations. Perhaps it actually looks like a key, perhaps it is an amulet or talisman that you would wear, or perhaps it is something else that is small and lightweight that you could carry with you at all times.

In your mind's eye, pick up the item. Visualise looking at it. Feel it, study it, describe it to yourself in words.

If it is something you can wear, then put it on. Otherwise, perhaps it is something to hold in your hand or put in a pocket. It is yours to keep and to take with you, so do so. Know that you will never be parted from this object in a guided visualisation unless you choose to be. If you drop it or put it down, it will return to you when you wish it. It is yours.

If, at any time, in any visualisation, you want to stop what is happening and be taken to your safe place, all you have to do is tell this item to take you there. It will do so – safely and fast.

In your mind's eye, look around you again. Visualise your safe place that you know you can come to when you want. But now, you are going to return to everyday reality.

Take a few deep breaths, in and out. Feel the solid surface beneath you. Wiggle your fingers and toes and return to your normal consciousness. When you are ready, open your eyes.

* * *

If you want, you can make notes afterwards. It might help you to draw a picture of your safe place, or describe it in words, so that you can remind yourself of what it is like. You can also draw your magical transportation key and have the picture with you at future times.

Before getting on with other things – particularly operating machinery or driving – make sure you are fully grounded in the real world. As I mentioned earlier, there are various ways of grounding. I like to have a cup of tea and a biscuit. Salty food can also be good as one of the best ways of bringing yourself to earth. But please don't eat or drink anything you shouldn't or don't want to consume. Another way of grounding is to press or stamp your feet on the ground a few times, or tap your fingers on a wooden, stone or metal surface – a table top is fine.

Things Revealed by the Tide

This guided visualisation uses as symbols for self-discovery the imagery of hidden things being revealed on a beach as the tide retreats.

* * *

Sit comfortably in a safe place before you start this guided visualisation. Close your eyes. Take several slow, deep breaths and relax. Visualise the following:

Imagine that you are at the coast, in a safe place, watching the sea from the top of a beach. The tide is high. Picture the scene in your mind and watch it for a while. Think of a question or something you have long wanted to find the answer to.

As the question forms itself in your mind, you notice the tide is going out. You continue to watch as it recedes.

More and more of the beach or shoreline is revealed. Look at it. What is it like? Is it rocky, sandy, pebbly?

You walk down the revealed land. It is still wet, but it is firm and safe underfoot. You follow the receding tide line, watching more and more be revealed. You study it as you walk. Spend some time looking at the shore at your feet as you go.

The tide goes out further and further – further than you have seen it go before. You see something special has been uncovered. Go up to it. It means something to you – something that can help you answer your question or guide you towards the answer.

Spend as much time as you need studying and learning from what has been revealed. If there is something for you to take, then take it. It is a treasure from the depths of the sea.

Then, return up the beach. When you have got back to the safe place at the top of the shoreline, you know it is time to return to everyday reality.

Take a few deep breaths, wiggle your fingers and toes, return to your normal consciousness and open your eyes.

The Seeds of Love

Love sometimes seems one of the most elusive things, and the loss of a loved one can be hard. But being in love is also the most wonderful feeling in the world. Here is a guided visualisation about love and the cycles of nature:

* * *

Sit comfortably and close your eyes. Relax. Take three deep breaths in and out, and visualise the following:

Let your mind turn to a time you felt love. Recall your strongest feelings of love. It could be feelings for someone you currently love, or someone from your past. It doesn't matter, so long as you can recall that feeling. Feel that love in your heart and let the feeling grow, filling your being with warmth and joy.

Without opening your eyes, cup your hands in front of you and visualise a tiny seed in your cupped hands. You have never seen a seed quite like it before. Visualise your love flowing through your arms and from your heart into that seed, infusing it with that warmth and joy. It is a seed of love.

Visualise in front of you a flower pot, full of rich, soft, dark earth. Then visualise yourself planting the seed into the pot and placing that pot somewhere where the sun will shine on it and the rain will water it.

Visualise the seed sprouting, a small shoot growing upwards, through the soil, into the light; and roots growing down, through the soil, to nourish and secure it. Watch it grow. A tiny fold of green leaves breaks through the soil and stretches upwards into the light and a network of roots grow below it in the dark soil.

A bud forms, a green sepal protecting the petals within. It is unique and beautiful. Watch as the bud opens, revealing tiny petals. The petals expand and open and become the most beautiful flower. It is a unique flower – you have never seen one exactly like it before. Examine the flower, its outer petals and inner stamen and pistil – the parts of the plant that let it reproduce.

Then, as you watch, a bee lands on the flower and enters the inner folds of the petals, brushing against the stamen in its search for the sweet nectar within, then re-emerging, flecked with pollen, and flying off on its busy way.

Look again at the flower, see how perfect it is. But, as you watch, the petals start to fade and wither. One by one they fall to the ground, and in their place grows a tiny fruit – different from the petals. You watch as it grows and ripens. It is unique, perfect and beautiful too.

But slowly the fruit softens, darkens and wrinkles, then it too falls from the plant and lands on the soil. It splits open, revealing inside seeds – many, many seeds. Seeds just like the one you held in your cupped hands and filled with love.

You collect the seeds and hold them in your cupped hands. Look at how many more there are than the one seed you started with. They are all precious seeds of love that you can plant, to grow, blossom, and flower to bring joy into the world.

Take three deep breaths in and out. Then open your hands, wiggle your fingers and toes and return to your normal consciousness. Open your eyes, but know that with this visualisation you can help plant seeds of love in the real world.

Fish in a Pond

Water can symbolise emotions and the subconscious. This could be a useful guided visualisation to do if you are seeking an answer within yourself to an emotional question.

* * *

Sit comfortably. Close your eyes and take three slow, deep breaths. Relax and visualise:

Imagine you are sitting beside a pond in a beautiful, peaceful garden. It is a warm day; the sun is shining, and the sky is blue with the occasional white fluffy cloud.

Around you, flowers are blooming, filling the garden with perfume. The grass is green and soft. The songs of birds can be heard. You look at the pond. There are water lilies on its surface and sunlight sparkles on the water. You feel relaxed and happy to be there.

Spend a little while enjoying being in the beautiful garden beside the pond.

After a while, a little cloud drifts in front of the sun, throwing a shadow over the garden. It feels suddenly cooler and sunlight no longer sparkles on the surface of the water in the pond.

For a moment, this disturbs you. Then you notice that without the light reflecting off the pond, you are able to see more clearly below the surface of the water. You realise the pond is deep and, although the bottom is lost in darkness, the water towards the top is clear even if tinged with green. You can see fronds of bright pondweed and water lily stalks stretching down into its depths.

Peering into the water, you glimpse a dark shape moving

somewhere far below the surface. It is a fish; a mottled silver-grey carp. As you watch, you see another, then another.

You realise that the pond is home to a shoal. This is their home – it is peaceful and cool, and they are happy to live there. Some seem to be at rest, only moving their gills as they take oxygen from the water. Others swim in a slow and graceful dance around each other. This glimpse into their watery world is so different from the land above.

Then, you notice one carp that is golden in colour, yet it swims in harmony with its grey-silver cousins.

Spend a little while watching the shoal of carp in the pond.

After a while, you realise that the golden carp has become aware of you. It seems to be watching you, as you are watching it. It rests for a moment, then slowly starts to swim upwards, towards the surface of the water, as though it wants to get a closer look at the human who is peering in from outside the pond.

As it gets close to the surface of the water, your eyes meet. There is an odd sense of understanding suddenly between you and the golden fish. You feel that it has a message for you; a secret it wants to tell you and you want to hear.

You bend down close to the surface of the water, as the fish rises up to just below the surface. Then, for a moment, the face of the golden carp breaks through the surface with a gentle splash and a ring of little bubbles.

Maybe you got the message it was trying to impart – perhaps in words, perhaps in images, perhaps just in your mind. Or perhaps it will come to you later.

The golden carp swims back down to the bottom of the pond to join its silver-grey cousins and you sit back up, beside the pond.

At that moment, the sun comes out from the other side of the cloud, its rays of light flooding the garden with warmth once more and sunlight sparkling from the pond surface.

Shortly you will return to your normal world, but for a little while longer stay in the garden and enjoy its beauty while pondering on the message from the golden carp.

Take three deep breaths in and out. Wiggle your fingers and toes and return to your normal consciousness. Open your eyes.

The Crystal of the Nine Eternities

This guided visualisation came to me in a dream. I hadn't heard of the Crystal of the Nine Eternities before and I don't know where my concept of it came from.

In my dream, the Crystal of the Nine Eternities is a shimmering crystal that is the colours of the rainbow (red, orange, yellow, green, blue, indigo and violet) plus black and white. It initially appears clear, but as you look, it can pass through all of these colours. Likewise, it can initially look like any gem or stone or object made of stone or crystal or even glass, but can change shape as you look at it and often appears like a glowing, shimmering, complex crystalline structure.

Think of the Crystal of the Nine Eternities as the ultimate scrying crystal, which can answer your questions or provide you with solutions to your problems. It represents hope, which is sometimes all we need to keep going when times are hard.

* * *

Sit comfortably, close your eyes, take a few deep breaths in out. Relax and visualise:

You are in a circle of stones, but know that you are going to leave the circle to go on a quest to find the Crystal of the Nine Eternities. Visualise the circle of stones and the location you are in. When you have looked all around you and taken in the sights and sounds, get ready to leave this area. Visualise moving away from the circle and exploring. Follow your heart, because your heart will lead you to the crystal. In your mind, go where your heart tells you to go. Somewhere, not too far away, is what you seek.

Initially, it might look like a perfectly ordinary object, although it is usually made of something that is stone, gem or crystal. It could be a pebble, or a glass chalice or a beautiful item of jewellery. You will know it when you see it because your heart will tell you. If it does, observe the item, it will start to glow and to shift form until you see in your mind's eye the most beautiful crystal you have ever seen – shimmering with light that is all the colours of the rainbow and maybe more. However, it could just as easily look just like that as soon as you see it. Ask it the question that is in your heart, and an answer will come to you. It might not come immediately, but it will.

Then, visualise a glowing replica of this crystal – a virtual Crystal of the Nine Eternities if you like. This replica moves from the object and into your body. It moves into your heart, merging with it and filling you with hope.

When you are ready, retrace your way to the circle of stones. Look around you again before getting ready to return to normal reality.

Take a few deep breaths in and out. Wiggle your fingers and toes, return to normal consciousness, then open your eyes.

Yule Tree Magic

This is an example of a creative visualisation, as it enables you to make a wish that might come true. It is designed to be done when decorating a tree for the winter festive season, whether you call it Christmas, Yule or the Solstice.

* * *

When you are ready to start, sit comfortably. Close your eyes, take three deep breaths in and out. Relax and visualise:
In your mind's eye, visualise a beautiful evergreen tree. Image

yourself dressing the tree with ornaments. Last of all, you place onto the tree a doll that looks like an angel or fairy or seasonal spirit.

You stand in front of the decorated tree and look at it. Look at the green branches and smell the scent of the pine needles. Admire your handiwork.

As you observe the tree, you can see the vibrant green energy of the deep earth going up into it, up through its roots and into its trunk, flowing along its branches.

You can also see silver energy from the heavens coming down and reaching the top of the tree, flowing all over its branches, down its trunk and into the earth at its roots.

You see the two streams of energy mingle and combine, suffusing everything on the tree and making it glow with light. As you watch, the energy flows into your doll, bringing them to life. They glow with energy.

You see that they have eyes and a mouth and other features on their face. They look at you and speak. 'Do you have a wish?' they ask you.

If you do, say what it is you wish for this Yuletide, and know that your wish will be heard by the angel, fairy or spirit of the season.

Spend a little more time conversing with them.

When you are ready, bring the conversation to an end. Say your goodbyes, but know that throughout this Yuletide, your doll and the tree and all that is on it will be filled with the magic of the season.

Take a few deep breaths in and out. Wiggle your fingers and toes, return to normal consciousness, then open your eyes.

Chapter 2

Guided Visualisations for the Wheel of the Year

I am a modern pagan witch and I celebrate and honour the changing seasons. I wrote the guided visualisations in this chapter in response to the energy, symbolism and magic of the festivals of the Wheel of the Year. In the northern hemisphere these are: Imbolc on February 1; Spring Equinox around March 21; Beltane on May 1; Summer Solstice around June 21; Lammas on August 1; Autumn Equinox around September 21; Samhain on October 31; and Winter Solstice around December 21. They are at the opposite times of the year in the southern hemisphere.

If you are following a contemporary pagan or earth-based spiritual path, then you can add these guided visualisations to your own celebrations, or use them to explore your own personal responses to the time of year. It is always good to have something to eat or drink after doing any psychic or magical work in order to ground properly. If you are including your visualisation as a Wheel of the Year ritual, then a feast of seasonal food would be particularly appropriate.

Imbolc: Waking up for Spring

Imbolc is the festival that celebrates the first signs of spring. Green shoots are pushing up from the soil and tree branches are tipped with sticky buds. Lambs are being born and some creatures that hibernate are starting to emerge from their winter sleep. Also, for humans, even though the weather can still be frosty, this can be when we start to shake off winter lethargy and plan for longer days ahead. This guided visualisation will help you tune into that energy.

* * *

Sit comfortably and close your eyes. Take three deep breaths in and out, relax, then visualise the following:

Imagine that you are lying under a warm, soft, dark, blanket. You are waking from a long sleep, but you are still drowsy. It is so comfortable here. You can feel no reason to move. Part of you wants to drift back to sleep again. Enjoy this liminal time between sleep and wakefulness.

After a while, you become aware of the sound of a bird singing somewhere outside your warm, dark, comfortable space. Listen to the bird song. It is beautiful. It sings the song again and again and you hear its joyous refrain. The song is about the morning and the new sun rising in a clear sky. Listen to the song.

It seems to call to you; to call you from your rest, and you feel a desire to emerge from your warm, dark, safe, place.

Visualise slowly stretching out and feeling your arms rise out of the soft, warm blanket. The air is cooler outside, but the stretch sends delicious tingles down your fingers, along your arms, through your shoulders and down your back.

You stretch out your legs, and feel the same delicious tingly sensation as your muscles move.

You feel the need to fill your lungs with fresh air. Stretch your neck and lift your head out from under the blanket. Take a deep breath and fill your lungs with cool, fresh air. You can smell the promise of spring in the air.

Visualise that you open your eyes. Through your mind's eye see the morning light shining on the ground. See the bird singing on a tree that is just ready to bud – buds that will soon sprout into tiny green leaves.

You get up and take in the scene. What do you see? Spend some time looking at the world and the signs of new life. Listen to the bird song and any other sounds you can hear. Smell the scents of the promise of spring. Feel the delicious sensation of your body alive once more after a long sleep. Spend more time enjoying the view, sounds and scents of this landscape.

When you are ready to end the visualisation, return to your normal reality. Take a real deep breath, shake your fingers and toes and open your eyes to the real world.

Spring Equinox: Balance – Seesaw in the Park

The spring equinox is when day and night are of equal length before hours of light become greater than those of darkness. In nature, spring flowers are blooming, there is blossom on the trees and green leaves are appearing.

For us, it can be a time to make changes to try to get our lives more in balance. This guided visualisation is to help with that. It is also good to do at other times of the year if you have had a disagreement with a friend or loved one and want to reconcile your differences.

* * *

Sit comfortably, relax and close your eyes. Take three deep breaths in and out, then visualise the following:

You are alone in a beautiful park in the springtime. It is a lovely day. The sun is shining and it is pleasantly warm. Spring flowers are blooming in the flowerbeds. There is blossom on the trees and small green leaves are beginning to bud. Birds are singing, some are flying overhead, and some are nesting. You feel safe and at ease here as you look around and explore the park.

As well as the trees and flowerbeds, the park has lawns, benches to sit on and paths to wander around and see the sights. Spend time looking at what there is around you.

After a while, you notice there is a seesaw in one part of the park. It might be old, but it is still working and completely safe to sit on. There is no one else around that you can see, but you decide to sit on one end of the seesaw.

You sit down. It is a good place to rest, but you cannot operate it on your own. You wish there was someone else to sit on the other end and make it work.

Your wish is granted as you see another figure moving down the path towards the seesaw. You realise they are someone you know – a friend or acquaintance, but one with whom you have had some difference of opinion, disagreement or argument in the past. Nevertheless, as they walk towards you, you see they are smiling both at you and at the seesaw.

They sit down on the other end, look at you and smile again.

Together you operate the seesaw without speaking. Both of you are enjoying the motion of pushing with your legs to soar up into the air and then gently descending, repeating the actions with innocent pleasure. You are both enjoying the spring in the park and playing on the seesaw with childlike joy.

Spend some time enjoying the seesaw.

When you are ready, let the seesaw come to a stop, perfectly in balance, with you sitting on one end and the other person on the other end.

The other person then speaks. They say they are glad to have met you in the park and ask if you would like to walk with them and talk.

Decide whether you want to. If you do not want to talk with them, then tell them so and they will accept what you say and politely leave you alone. If you do want to talk with them, then you both get off the seesaw and walk together around the park.

Spend some time walking and talking. Be aware of how the conversation moves between you and see if eventually you can find some balance in what you are discussing.

Eventually bring your conversation to an end. You both say goodbye to each other. Do that in whatever way seems best before they turn and walk away from you, out of the park.

When you are ready to end the visualisation, return to normal reality. Take a deep breath, shake your fingers and toes, and open your eyes to the real world.

Beltane Eve: The Path to Love

Beltane Eve is a traditional time for doing divination to see the face of a future lover, to scry into the spirit world to meet lovers who have passed on, or for any magic relating to love. This guided visualisation involves meeting a lover past, present or future in your mind's eye.

* * *

Sit comfortably, relax and close your eyes. Take three deep breaths in and out, then visualise the following:

It is just before dusk on Beltane Eve. You are in an old English village. It is the kind of traditional village that has not changed for centuries. This is somewhere you feel completely safe and at ease. There is a green in the centre of the village and on it people have been setting things up for the May Day festivities that will start tomorrow morning. A maypole has been erected, with coloured ribbons, where people will dance. In other places, there are preparations for fun and games.

Around the village green are cottages with gardens full of spring flowers. There is an inn too. Its lights are on and you can hear the sound of people beginning to celebrate inside.

Just as you are about to join them, you hear your name called from another direction. The sound is faint, almost a whisper, or a long way away, but the voice seems familiar. It is the voice of someone you love, or have loved, or someone you will love. It is the voice of a lover.

You turn around and look in the direction the sound is coming from. Where you look, there is a lane leading past the cottages at the edge of the green and out of the village.

Perhaps there is a moment of indecision, but you hear the

voice again. Even if you are not sure exactly who the voice belongs to, it is a voice you want to follow. You decide to do so. Walking across the green, you step onto the lane and continue along it past the cottages and out of the village.

There are high hedgerows on either side of the lane, which are full of hawthorn blossom and new green leaves. You follow the lane and at the end you find a gate. Beyond the gate you can see an apple orchard. The trees are in full blossom. You hear your lover's voice calling you again. They are calling from within the apple orchard. You open the gate, and go through, into the orchard.

Apple trees are all around you, their branches thickly covered in white blossom. A narrow path winds into the orchard, and on either side of the path, below the trees, the orchard floor is a carpet of bluebells.

You follow the path as it winds through the trees until you come to the centre.

In the centre of the orchard stands the oldest of the apple trees. Its branches spread out wide and are high enough that you can easily walk beneath them. Sitting on a bench, at the foot of the apple tree, you see your lover. Your eyes meet and they smile at you and once more say your name in a way that you know means they are happy you are here, that you have heard them, and came to them.

You join your lover beneath the tree. Spend time with them.

Dusk grows and the sky gets darker, but a full moon rises beyond the apple orchard. There is enough light to see and the evening is warm enough to stay outside as long as you desire.

Eventually, your lover says they must go, for they have things to do before the morning of the first of May. You know it is time for you to leave too. You say your good-byes, but your lover promises that, if you want, they will meet you again.

You return along the path through the orchard, through the gate, along the lane and back to the village where everything is prepared for Beltane morn.

When you are ready to end the visualisation, return to normal reality. Take a deep breath, shake your fingers and toes, and open your eyes to the real world.

Summer Solstice: The Sun Temple

Many ancient sites throughout the world align with the summer solstice. Although most of the UK's megalithic monuments align primarily to the winter solstice, some – including Bryn Celli Ddu in Wales – have a summer alignment. In this guided visualisation you imagine you are travelling to a temple sacred to the sun.

You can visualise a temple anywhere you like. It can be one that exists now, one that used to exist, or one from your own imagination. Before starting, you can think about where you want to visit, or just see what comes to you. The guided visualisation also offers an opportunity to make a promise, vow or dedication, so you might also want to think about whether you would like to do that at this time.

* * *

Sit comfortably, relax and close your eyes. Take three deep breaths in and out, then visualise the following:

Visualise that you are walking on a sacred route through a landscape, travelling to a temple sacred to the sun on the day of the summer solstice. Look around you, what landscape are you travelling through? What is the path like? Are you alone, or are others travelling with you? What do you see? What do you hear? What do you smell?

Observe what is around you on your journey as you travel to the Temple of the Sun.

After a while, you see you are starting to approach the temple. You see it in the distance at first, on the horizon, but appearing to grow larger as you move towards it. What does it look like? How does the landscape change? What sounds, sights and smells are there now?

Walk on, towards the temple. Visualise your approach until you stand before its outer boundaries.

Look up at the temple. What does it look like? What is happening? What are the sounds and smells of this place?

You see the entrance to the temple is guarded. Only those who pass their scrutiny and behave appropriately will be allowed to pass. Spend some time preparing yourself.

When you are ready, walk up to the entrance guardian. Greet them and ask what is necessary to enter the temple. Answer their questions and decide if you will do what is asked of you to pass through into the temple. This is your last point to turn back, should you wish to.

If you do as is asked, you pass the scrutiny of the guardian and pass through the entrance.

What sights do you see inside? Look around, look down, look up. Then, find the way inwards to the sacred space at the heart of the temple.

You enter the sacred space where the sun will align at the moment of the solstice. You have arrived in time, and must now wait. Look around you. Are you in light or darkness? What can you see? What can you hear? What can you smell? Are others with you? What do you do as you wait?

Slowly a focused ray of light from the sun enters the temple, moving over the ground and highlighting the features of this sacred space. What does it look like? What is happening? Watch and do what you know is the right thing at this time and in this place.

The sun reaches its zenith. For a moment it seems as though the sun is standing still, as though time is standing still, as though you are connected through space and time to all those who have been in the sun's sacred space in the past and in the future. It is a magical moment, perhaps a time to make a vow, a promise or a dedication to a spiritual path. If you wish to do so, do so now.

At last, the stretched moment ends. The ray of sunlight starts to move again over the ground. You watch as its last focused ray leaves the area of the sacred space.

It is time to leave. You walk out of the space and through the temple, back to the entrance. You pass the guardian and leave the temple behind you. You head back along the route you travelled, to the place you started from. Stop and look around you once more at the landscape, then prepare to return to normal reality.

When you are ready to end the visualisation, return to normal reality. Take a deep breath, shake your fingers and toes, and open your eyes to the real world.

Lammas: The Wise Woman's Cottage

Lammas is the festival of the first fruits of the harvest, at the time of year when grain crops are brought in. It can traditionally be celebrated by baking bread. Whether you have the skills, ingredients or inclination for cooking or not, here's a guided visualisation you can do.

* * *

Find somewhere safe, where you will not be disturbed. Sit comfortably and close your eyes. Take three deep breaths in and out and relax, then visualise the following:

Visualise that you are in a baker's shop, in a small village in the countryside. It is Lammas, when the fields are ripe, and the crops are brought in. You have been asked to deliver a basket of freshly baked bread to an old woman who lives on her own in a cottage on edge of the village, beyond the first field.

Taking the basket, you walk out of the door of the baker's shop and into the village street. It is a hot, dry, sunny day. Your journey takes you first along a street of old cottages, with gardens full of flowers.

At the end of the street there is a fence with a stile and beyond that a field golden with ripe grain. You cross the stile and enter the field. A path leads around the edge of the field. You see poppies and other wild flower and herbs growing in the borders. Beyond that you see a grain crop being harvested under the hot sun.

You watch the ripe grain being cut down in neat rows as you walk along the path. Crows circle in the sky above, and perhaps you catch a glimpse of other birds or animals. In the distance the farmer steadily harvests the crops, absorbed in his work. Observe what is happening as you walk along the path.

At the far end of the field is an old hedge. After a while you reach it. In the hedge is a gate, which leads into the old woman's garden behind her cottage. Open the gate and walk into the garden, carefully closing the gate again behind you.

The garden at first seems overgrown. With trees at the sides, shrubs and bushes and tall plants, it offers cool, dappled shade from the sun. You make your way further into the garden and see flowers growing everywhere. It is full of bright colours. Bees are going from flower to flower, birds are singing and there are sign of other wildlife too.

You then see the old woman. She is harvesting berries and putting them into a basket. You go up to her and greet her. She smiles and greets you in reply, then invites you in to her cottage. She opens the door and you follow her inside.

The old woman invites you to sit at her table and put down the basket of bread, then she offers you tea. She prepares the tea using leaves in an earthenware teapot, and brings out a jar of fresh jam she has made from her garden berries, and butter and milk she tells you is from a neighbour's farm.

You join her for tea. The fresh bread, butter and jam are delicious. You talk with her as you enjoy your tea together. What do you talk about?

When you have finished your tea, she asks if you would like her to divine your future or answer a question, by reading the patterns in the leaves at the bottom of your cup. If you do, let her see the cup.

She turns it three times clockwise and then holds it to the sunlight that streams through the cottage window. Then she answers your question and gives you an idea of what the future might possibly hold for you. If you want, she can show you the patterns in the leaves and how she has interpreted them.

Then it is time for you to leave. You say goodbye and stand up, picking up the empty bread basket. As you are about to go, the old woman presses a final gift into your hands. You look at it and thank her, then put the gift into the basket and wave goodbye as you go out of the cottage door.

You walk back through her garden, through the gate in the hedge, along the path at the edge of the field and over the stile into the village. You walk back along the street and return the basket to the bakery shop, where you began your journey. You may keep the gift the old woman gave you, and remember the things she told you.

When you are ready, take a deep breath, shake your fingers and toes and open your eyes to the real world.

* * *

After this visualisation, you could have a harvest feast – or just some fresh bread and jam and a cup of tea.

Autumn Equinox: The Autumn Garden
The equinoxes are when day and night are of equal length and they happen in both the spring and the autumn. Here is a guided visualisation celebrating the mellow season.

* * *

Sit comfortably and close your eyes. Take three deep breaths in and out and relax, then visualise the following:

You are in a garden. It is late afternoon at that time of year which, on golden days, you can still believe is late summer, yet you know is autumn. The sun is shining. When you stand in its brightness, you can feel it warming your skin, yet in long shadows that stretch across the lawn, you can feel a chill touch you.

The trees and hedges still have plenty of green leaves, yet there are patches of red, yellow and brown among them, and some leaves fallen to the ground. There are bright berries, too, although much of the fruit has already been picked. Around you, flowers are still blooming. Perhaps you see purple Michaelmas daisies, late roses or others. You also see that many have gone to seed. Brown stalks stand among others in the garden.

Spend some time exploring the garden. What do you see? What do you smell? What do you hear? What do you feel?

While examining the things in the garden, you spot a creature that seems to be observing you. The creature does not seem afraid of your presence. They seem to be aware that you have seen them, but do not move away.

What is the creature? What do they look like?

They look at you steadily, and you get the impression they are inviting you to move closer.

You slowly and quietly move closer to the creature. They remain still, looking at you, until you are right in front of them.

What does the creature want? Does the creature need your help, or are they offering something for you?

Spend some time with the creature, interacting with them in the way that seems right.

After some time, the creature indicates that they must go. They turn and leave you in the garden.

Looking around, you realise that the shadows have lengthened. It is early evening and time for you to leave the autumn garden too.

When you are ready, take a deep breath, shake your fingers and toes and open your eyes to the real world.

Halloween or Samhain: A Visitor from the Past

Whether you celebrate Halloween or Samhain, the festival that marks the first signs of winter is a time to think about those who have passed on. The festivals and celebrations at this time of year are also when we traditionally celebrate things we find scary, such as dark nights and spooky stories. This guided visualisation aims to help you tune into that energy. I should warn you; this is not intended to be entirely safe or comfortable. It could be scary. I would particularly recommend reading through the text before doing the visualisation to assess whether you want to do it or not.

* * *

Find somewhere safe and comfortable. Sit and close your eyes. Take three deep breaths in and out and relax, then visualise the following:

Visualise that you are in a room where you feel comfortable and safe. Perhaps it is a room in your own home, a room you recall from your past, or a place created in your imagination as being the most wonderfully safe and comfortable place in the world. The room is pleasantly warm and well lit, as outside it is night. The room has a place for you to sit and be at ease, a table where you can rest things, a door and a window or windows securely shut against the night. Around you are things you like.

You are contently seated in the chair and can relax. Everything you need at this moment is here. Look around the room. Visualise it. Enjoy it.

Then, suddenly, the window rattles. The lights go out. You are in darkness. You hear strange noises outside and know there is something out there. Something would like to come in.

Yet, this room is safe. You know that. The door and windows are securely shut. Surely what is outside, cannot come inside unless you let it – can it? Slowly your eyes adjust to the gloom. You can just make out the outlines of what is in the room by faint starlight in the night sky through the window. Familiar things in the room appear as dark shapes. You can see the edges of the chair you are in. You can see the table.

You get up and try to put the lights back on, but the room remains in darkness.

Then you realise there are some things on the table you do not recall being there earlier. There is a candle in a candlestick, and the means to light it. There is also a crystal ball, next to it.

You light the candle. Its wick splutters, then the flame becomes strong. Its light illuminates a circle around it, falling gently across the crystal ball. The rest of the room is still only dimly lit, but the room seems still safe. The door and the windows are still closed against the blackness outside.

You sit at the table with the candle, then you notice something flicker within the crystal ball. You move the crystal closer to the candle so the light falls on it. You look into the ball. What you see in it is not your own reflection or a reflection of the room. Instead, you see a person. Someone who is not you, but who you feel you recognise from the past. Perhaps someone who has passed beyond the veil of life. Perhaps they are an ancestor you have only seen pictures of in the past, perhaps they are someone you have imagined meeting, but who lived long ago.

As you look at the person in the crystal, you realise they are looking back at you. Your eyes meet and you are certain that they can see you as well as you can see them.

Then, they speak. You can see their lips move, and it is as though you can hear the words they are saying in your mind.

Hear what they say. What do you say to them in reply?

Spend time conversing with this person. Tell them things you want to say and listen to the words they say to you. Ask them things you want to ask, and hear what they reply.

After you have been conversing with the person in the crystal for a while, you realise the candle light is dimming. The flame has burnt low. Say your last few words of conversation with the person from the past and say your goodbyes now.

The candle goes out. You are plunged in darkness once more. You hear sounds outside the room, outside the windows and door, of someone walking away into the blackness of the night. Then, all is quiet.

You sit for a moment in the dark room in silence, then the lights come back on. Not the candle light, but the light that was illuminating the room at first. You glance at the table. The candlestick and crystal ball are not there anymore, but the room is back to the way it was when you first visualised it. The room is safe and warm and comfortable. The door and the windows are securely shut. Look around you and see that all is returned to normal.

When you are ready take a deep breath, shake your fingers and toes and open your eyes to the real world.

* * *

I always recommend grounding properly after a visualisation. That is particularly important if you done work that has led you to face fears or contemplate anything unsettling.

Winter Solstice Eve: Past, Present and Future

This visualisation is inspired by Charles Dickens' classic seasonal story *A Christmas Carol*, in which the protagonist meets the ghosts of Christmas past, present and future, but gives it a pagan twist.

* * *

Find somewhere safe and comfortable. Sit and close your eyes. Take three deep breaths in and out and relax, then visualise the following:

Visualise that you are warmly in bed. It is late on winter solstice eve and you are ready to go to sleep. Just as you are about to drift off into slumber, you hear a distant clock strike 11. The sound wakes you. You are unsure where the sound is coming from, as you have not heard that clock strike before. Then, you hear knocking at your front door.

You get out of bed, wrap yourself warmly, and go to the door. Outside is an old man, stooped with age, carrying a lantern. He addresses you by name and tells you that you have been chosen for a special invitation, to follow him and to learn the secrets of the past, the present and the future.

You see that outside; all is frosty, and everything seems to glisten in the moonlight. Your breath turns to fog in the chill air.

If you choose to go, put on your boots and coat follow him from your house. He leads you along a deserted road that is at first familiar, but seems to change as you go. The familiar sights and landmarks that you know fade and, in their place, rise tall, wintry trees. You are walking through a wood on a winding path. Your feet crunch on fallen leaves and twigs underfoot. The old man's lamp lights the way, but around its circle of light is darkness.

He leads you on to a clearing. In that clearing, three figures move around a huge cauldron on a bright, warm fire. Steam rises from the cauldron. As you get closer you see that one of the figures is an old woman with a lined face and wise eyes, the second is a woman with a motherly face and kind eyes, the third figure is a youth, with an innocent face, but sad eyes.

The old man explains these are the spirits of the past, the present and the future and each in turn will show you something important.

First the old woman throws into the bubbling cauldron

dark leaves of an evergreen tree, and from the steam that arises you start to see a vision. It is a vision of the past – something important to you. Watch it unfold.

Eventually, the vision ends.

The old man speaks: 'What you have seen is in the past. The past cannot be changed, but we can remember and learn from what has taken place.'

Then the motherly woman throws into the cauldron a handful of red holly berries. In the steam you see visions of the present. These are scenes from your everyday life that, even if you had not realised it before, are important. You watch the scenes as they unfold.

After a while, the vision ends, and the old man speaks: 'What you have seen is still ongoing. Everything you do and say is important, even if you do not realise it. What you do now affects what will happen in the future. The future is what you will see next.'

Then the youth with sad eyes throws white berries of mistletoe into the cauldron. Steam arises from it and in the steam, you see a vision of the future. You watch the scene unfold.

Before the scene is over, the old man speaks. 'What you see is only one possible future, but it is likely to come to pass unless your actions change the course of time.'

The vision of the future unfolds further, then fades. All you see is steam arising from the cauldron over the glowing fire, and the three spirits beyond it, watching you, but saying nothing.

The old man speaks again: 'It is time for you to return home, and to sleep. Tomorrow is the winter solstice. It is the shortest day of the year, but know that the actions you take, or promises that you make in the light of the returning sun, will affect how the future unfolds.'

He leads you back along the winding forest path. Slowly the trees around you start to fade and you see familiar sights and landmarks around your home. The old man returns with you to your front door, and bids you farewell. You can exchange some final words with him, before you go inside and close the door. You take off your coat and boots and return to your bed. You pull up the covers and close your eyes. In the distance you hear a bell ring, but you do not hear how many tolls it makes, whether it is still in the eleventh hour or whether it has struck midnight, because you have already fallen into a deep and dreamless sleep.

When you are ready, take a deep breath, shake your fingers and toes and open your eyes to the real world.

* * *

If you do make any promises or resolve to take any actions, make a note of them to remind yourself in the New Year.

Chapter 3

The Power of the Moon

Witchcraft is often done under the light of the full moon, because its energy lends itself to magic and spellwork. Here is a guided visualisation to do at that powerful time in the moon's monthly cycle.

Full Moon Visualisation

Find somewhere safe and comfortable. Sit and close your eyes. Take three deep breaths in and out and relax, then visualise the following:

Imagine you are in the main room of an old-fashioned cottage, perhaps the cottage of a wise woman or wise man from the past. Imagine that it is your cottage and you are the wise person. Your cottage is sparsely furnished, but comfortable, with an open fireplace and a besom broom propped against the back door. It is dusk. The room is lit by the glow from the fire and a lantern which hangs on a hook from a ceiling beam, but you can still see a little light through the window at the front. The window looks out onto a small garden leading to a country lane bordered by an ancient hedge. Beyond the hedge there is a hill, silhouetted in the twilight sky.

On a hook on the wall by the front door of the cottage hangs a warm cloak and next to that is propped a wooden staff. Take the cloak and put it on, then take the lantern and staff and leave the cottage by the front door.

Walk down your garden path and into the country lane. Past your garden, the hedge rises high on either bank of the lane. You cannot see what lies the other side. You walk for a while, aware of your footsteps and the sounds, sights and scents of the country lane in the early evening.

After some time, you come to a tall gate in the hedge. It is an old gate, worn by the elements – the gales of spring, the sun of high summer, the storms of autumn and the frosts of winter. Yet it is still sturdy and closed to all except those who know the way to open it, such as yourself. You know how to open the gate and you do so. Pay attention to how easily or difficult it, the stiffness of the mechanism, the weight of the gate.

The gate opens and you step through.

On the other side, a path slopes gently upwards into a dark wood. Night has encroached, and only the glow of your lantern illuminates a few steps ahead. You must tread carefully.

The path continues through the trees, but the way is not easy. Fallen branches and twisted roots are obstacles hard to see in the darkness. You hear sounds around you – wind in the branches, rustling in the undergrowth, a distant bark, a hoot. Twigs at the ends of branches catch at your clothing. Find your way through the dark wood, but beware of dangers, and keep to the path.

You follow the path through the dark forest for some time.

Eventually you notice the trees start to thin and ˙silvery moonlight shines between the trunks and through gaps in the branches overhead. The path is illuminated by the moonlight now and leads you safely out of the woods.

Once out of the trees, you see the hill rise in front of you – a high mound with grassy slopes and a ring of trees at the top.

The path continues. It spirals up the hillside, around and around. There are no obstacles here except the incline. You will need perseverance to make it to the top. You have your staff to lean on, and progress up the hill, around the twisting path.

As you round the bends in the spiral, ascending the hill, the path takes you up above the canopy of the forest. The moon has risen. It is a full moon. It shines brightly in a clear, starry sky. You stop to catch your breath. As you pause in your journey, you look around. You see the landscape stretched out below, distant. It is the world you left behind when you walked through the gate. The path ahead looks steeper still, but you go on.

You continue on the path as the spirals get steeper and climb higher, towards the top of the hill. The hilltop is crowned by a ring of dense, ancient trees, which you approach although the last curve of the path is the steepest. You round the last, steep bend and see before you an opening in the ring of trees, a gateway to the top of the hill.

You step through the gap into the circle within.

The moon's silvery light shines down and illuminates the ground within the circle of trees. In the centre is a dew pond, full of collected water, reflecting the bright, full moon in the starry sky above.

You walk towards the pond and look into it. You can see in the water the image of the silver disc of the moon and the image of your own reflection. Then you see a third image; that of a being standing next to you.

For a moment, you are surprised. How did they get here? Where did they come from? Who are they? Then you realise you know who they are, even if you have not met them before.

Turn to face them. Greet them. Talk to them.

Spend some time conversing with them. Say what you need to say and listen to what they reply in return. Perhaps they have a message for you.

After a while, your conversation comes to an end. The being you are talking to tells you to look once more into the pool. You do and once more see the reflection of the moon – now directly overhead. You see the reflection of your own face too. But the being you met is no longer reflected there. They are gone.

You know it is time for you to leave too; to return home.

You retrace your steps to the gap in the circle of trees, down the spiral path around the hillside and into the dark wood. Now the wood does not seem so frightening. You easily find your way through it to the old gate in the hedge. You open the gate and pass through it to the lane, shutting the gate carefully behind you. Then you walk back along the lane, up your garden path and into your cottage. You close the door, replace your staff and lantern and hang up your cloak. Your journey is complete.

When you are ready take a deep breath, shake your fingers and toes and open your eyes to the real world.

Chapter 4

Visualisations for the Elements

One of the first lessons in many witchcraft traditions is to gain an understanding of the elements: earth, air, fire and water. The elements are often called upon to lend their aid to spells being cast and rituals performed. These guided visualisations were written with that in mind; to help trainee witches become familiar with each element and develop a personal awareness of what they represent or symbolise. These elemental guided visualisations can also be done to become more in balance with the natural world.

Earth

Find somewhere safe and comfortable. Sit and close your eyes. Take three deep breaths in and out and relax, then visualise the following:

Visualise that you are outside in a familiar place on a fine day. It is a place you have come before to sit and rest. It is a pleasant spot that you like, where you feel safe and at ease. Spend a few moments taking in the familiar surroundings. Listen to the sounds, smell any scents and quietly observe.

After a little while you spot something you have not noticed before. It is an opening – perhaps a doorway or an entrance, a gap in a wall or a gate, perhaps it is a hole in the ground. It is open and you are curious. You get up and take a closer look at this entranceway. You have an urge to go through it and see what is inside, but possibly that curiosity is mixed with caution. Examine your feelings and resolve them before going through the entrance.

Inside, a short passageway leads to steps going down. You go along the passageway and down the steps. They go down a long way.

At the bottom of the steps, you find yourself facing another passage. Ahead in the distance you can see a small, faint light source, but the space from where you are until you reach that small light source is in darkness. You will have to go through that. Plucking up your courage you step into the darkness.

How do you proceed? What is the passage like? What sounds are there? What smells? What does it feel like underfoot and, if you touch the sides of the passage, what do they feel like? Take as much time as you need to get through it.

You eventually reach the source of the small illumination and find a portable light that you can take with you. Pick it up. Looking ahead now, you realise you are underground. Around you, you can see evidence of past human endeavour in this underground system hewn from rock or dug into the earth.

Carrying your light source, you continue further into this area. You observe the past achievements of human beings, preserved within the earth. Take your time to explore. There is a lesson from the past to be seen here. Think about what it means to you and what you can learn from it.

When you feel you have spent enough time exploring the underground area with its evidence of human endeavour, you come to a cleft in the solid walls of rock or stone or earth, with a narrow passageway beyond it, once more going downwards. Squeeze through into the passageway, which slopes downwards.

This passage is different from the area you have just explored. It is part of a natural cave, unaltered by man. You travel onwards and as your light illuminates the surface of the rock, you become aware of its texture, colour and consistency – its mineral structure and the way it was formed give it a unique appearance. As you move onwards through this passage, you learn secrets of the past from this stone. You continue, observing the cave as you go, seeking to understand its message. The further and deeper you go, the more the message becomes clear. Travel at your own pace and decipher the message of the stone.

After some time, you come to another narrow cleft. You cannot see what lies at the other side of this tiny way through, or how long it goes on for. You can see that to get through this will be a tight squeeze. The opening is so narrow it will be difficult to get in and you do not know if it gets narrower. You also realise that cannot see what lies beyond, even when you hold your light up to the opening.

Decide whether you want to go on.

If you decide not to risk it, you may return the way you came, back through the cave and passage, then up the stairs and through to the safe place in which you began your journey. If you do that, end this visualisation there.

If you decide to continue forward, you must consider the gap and the best way to attempt to squeeze through the narrow opening. Make your decision now.

If you decide to go on, you squeeze into the gap. You struggle and at times it feels as though you are stuck. In the cramped, tight space, your light source goes out. You are constricted and in darkness, but you struggle on.

Eventually, with much effort, you manage to get through. And you realise it was worth it.

You find yourself in the most awe-inspiring cavern you have ever seen. It is lit by some strange glow from within the rocks themselves. Natural wonders glisten on every surface. Look around.

You become aware you are not alone. At the far end of the cavern you see a figure you know to be an earth elemental. You are in their realm. Cross the cavern and go to the elemental creature. Approach them and greet them.

The earth elemental replies, speaking words meant for you alone. Listen to what they have to say, and converse with them.

After a while, your conversation draws to a close. You thank the elemental for what you have learnt and what you have seen.

The elemental beckons you forward again, and hands you a gift, for you to take with you, back to your realm above the ground. You look to see what the gift is, as it is placed into your hand.

As you look at the gift, you become aware of a change around you. When you look up you realise that you have returned to your safe and familiar spot above the ground, where you started this visualisation.

When you are ready take a deep breath, shake your fingers and toes and open your eyes to the real world.

Air

Find somewhere safe and comfortable. Sit and close your eyes. Take three deep breaths in and out and relax, then visualise the following:

You are in a garden at the foot of a steep hill. It is a beautiful garden, full of flowers and with pleasant places to sit. A gentle breeze is blowing, wafting the fragrance of the blooms and the other scents of the garden. In the sky, the sun is shining through gaps in the clouds and it is pleasantly warm. Sit in the garden for a while and look around at the flowers. Smell their fragrance, feel the gentle breeze on your face and in your hair. Spend some time enjoying the garden.

After a while, the sun slowly disappears behind the clouds. The sky is growing grey and overcast.

You feel you no longer wish to just sit in the garden. Looking around, you spot a gate at the end of the garden, leading to a path that winds up the hill. You decide to go for a walk.

Make your way to the gate, open it, and step onto the path.

The path is on a gentle incline. It gradually circles around the hill, ascending slowly. You walk along it. As you go, look to either side of the path, what do you see?

Spend some time continuing on the path, up the hill.

After a while, you realise the clouds are lowering as you climb. You are walking into mist. You can see the path at your feet, a little way ahead and to either side, but any further is obscured by fog.

You make your way up the hill and find the path is growing steeper. You become more aware of your own breathing as the journey becomes harder. You know you are still safe, but it is tough going.

For a while, all is grey and foggy. Then you see lighter mist ahead of you and know you will pass through the upper layers of the cloud.

Suddenly, you are out of the fog. The path has ascended above the cloud layer. The sky above is brilliant clear blue and below you is a white carpet of clouds. Above you, the pathway ascends to the top of the hill, but it is still steep. You carry on climbing and at last you make it to the top. You stop to catch your breath. You look down and see the clouds and fog below have gone. The view is amazing.

Below you, you can see familiar places you have left behind, and the path you took. You feel a sense of achievement in getting this far. Then you realise you are not alone on the hilltop. Hovering in the air, there is a being or creature. They look at you. Then they speak. They say they are an air elemental and that if you want, they can grant you – temporarily – the power to fly into the air.

You must make a decision. Should you approach the being or creature and take up the offer of flight, or should you remain firmly on the ground of the hilltop?

If you decide to accept the air elemental's offer, listen to what they have to say as they explain to you the means of travelling upwards into the sky.

You thank them for their advice, and then decide whether to do what you have been told. If you choose to go ahead with the flight, make the necessary preparations to take that leap of faith before launching into the air. If you choose not to take the offered gift of flight, you must return down the hill on foot, by the path you ascended.

If you are willing to accept the offered gift of flight, once you have prepared yourself, you leave the ground behind you. You stay aloft. You fly. You soar.

Moving through the air, you see the ground below you grow smaller as you rise higher.

Spend time swooping, soaring, flying in the air and exploring the skies.

Eventually, you see the air elemental again. They fly beside you and tell you it is time to return to the ground as your powers of flight cannot continue forever.

But, before you land, they say they have something to tell you. Listen to what the air elemental has to say.

You thank the air elemental and say goodbye, then feel yourself drifting slowly and gently downwards. You see below you the garden in which you began your adventure. It is getting closer and closer, larger and larger. Gently you land back on the ground and realise that your powers of flight have ended. You are safe and well back where you started.

When you are ready, take a deep breath, shake your fingers and toes and open your eyes to the real world.

Fire

Find somewhere safe and comfortable. Sit and close your eyes. Take three deep breaths in and out and relax, then visualise the following:

You are in your bed in a safe and familiar place, but it is before dawn. This is a special day and you have awoken in the dark. You have a journey ahead of you – a long journey on foot. This is something you feel passionate about doing although you know it will be an ordeal.

You know the path you will set out on, but do not know exactly where it will end, or what you will encounter along the way. You light a single candle, to dress by.

Spend a few moments thinking about how you will prepare '
yourself for the day and what you will wear for your journey.

When you are ready, blow out your candle and leave your safe and familiar place. As you step out into the open, you see the first rays of the sun's light on the horizon. You watch as the glow begins to spread into the sky in the east and you start your journey.

You are travelling along a pathway as the sun rises. You continue for a long while, the light and heat of the day increasing. Be aware of what is around you – the road, the landscape, the sights, the sounds and the smells.

The journey is long, and you begin to feel hot and tired, yet you desire to continue your journey. You travel on for many miles, as the sun rises higher in the sky until it is directly overhead. The air above the ground on the path ahead of you begins to shimmer from the heat. The heat haze forms what seems like a translucent and flickering curtain across your path that obscures the way ahead. It is a barrier of light and heat that you must pass through.

Perhaps you have a moment's trepidation before passing through this barrier, which seems like a gateway to the unknown. But you know you must pass through it, so you do.

On the other side of the heat haze, the landscape has changed. It seems rocky and volcanic. It is hot. Yet the pathway continues onwards and you continue your journey.

After a while you see a figure ahead of you, standing in the middle of the path. The figure waves at you, as though they wish to attract your attention. You stop to talk to them.

The figure tells you the road ahead, just out of sight, is broken by a fissure. They say the road is dangerous, and you should turn back. What do you say or do?

If you take their advice and turn back, then you return to your safe and familiar place. Perhaps you will try the journey again another time or in another way.

If you decide to continue your journey, you leave the figure behind you and continue on to the break in the road.

It seems as though movement of the land or an earthquake has cracked the road. A long fissure lies across it and steam or smoke wafts up through the cleft. There does not appear to be an easy way around this fissure, which stretches in either direction across your path. There is nothing you can see to bridge the gap, as the land is rocky and bare.

The only way across is to jump. You are confident that you could safely do that jump, but it will require courage. Spend a few moments deciding what to do. Once again, if you decide to turn back you can do so and return to the safe place where you started your day. The rest of this described journey is not for you.

If you decide to jump, spend some time making your preparations, then leap.

As soon as you jump, you suddenly realise you are safe and will make it across to the other side.

You survived the leap and assess the way ahead. Once again you can see a way forward, a path leading towards your destination. You travel on for much time.

Look at the road and observe the landscape. What is it like?

The sun is now beginning to set ahead of you. The sky darkens as the sun lowers towards the horizon. As the twilight deepens, you see ahead of yourself, to the side of the road, a large bonfire.

As you get closer to it, you see that, around the fire, figures are dancing in celebration.

The figures wave at you and beckon you over. You feel the urge to join the dancers and join in the dance. You join their circle around the fire, learning the steps of the dance and joining in the celebration.

Eventually you know you must continue your journey. When you are ready, take your leave of the dancers and continue your journey by the light of the moon.

After a while, you see that the path ahead has an added hazard for it is covered in hot, glowing coals. You must walk over them. You know that glowing coals can be walked over without burning you. You take that first brave step, putting your feet on the smouldering coals, yet find that you are safe. You are unharmed by the fire, though you may feel its heat.

You walk on, seeing shapes and shadows in the glowing coals and flickering flames. These shapes and shadows may have significance for you. As you walk over them at an even pace, observe what they show you.

You approach the end of the burning pathway and a curtain of fire rises before you. You have no option but to pass through it, feeling its flames flicker over you, leaving you unharmed, but burning away your fears and misgivings.

You are at the other side. You find you are in a circle surrounded by a curtain of fire. You are safe and comfortable, but fire and flames are all around the edges of the space. You know your ordeal is behind you and you are at your destination.

At the far side of the circle you see a figure you know to be the elemental of fire. You approach them and greet them.

The elemental replies, speaking words meant for you alone. Listen to what they say, and converse with them.

Your conversation finally draws to a close. The elemental then hands you a gift. Look to see what the gift is, as it is placed into your hand. You thank the fire elemental and say goodbye. Then you become aware of a change around you. The air shimmers and then clears. You look up you realise that you have returned to your safe and familiar place, where you started your journey early that day.

When you are ready take a deep breath, shake your fingers and toes and open your eyes to the real world.

Water

Find somewhere safe and comfortable. Sit and close your eyes. Take three deep breaths in and out and relax, then visualise the following:

You are sitting comfortably beside a natural spring, where

water bubbles from the ground into a pool. The place you are sitting feels peaceful and safe. It is a lovely day. Sit here for a few moments, watching the water and listening to the sounds and scents.

The spring is the source of a stream that runs beyond this safe and peaceful place, and you have decided to set out on a journey down that stream, to its end, on a voyage of discovery. As a final gesture before you set off, take a small item of value, something that is yours and which you have on you, and throw it into the pool, making a wish for a safe journey as you watch it splash into the surface of the water, then descend into its depths.

You are now ready to depart on your journey. Gather any few things you want to take with you, walk through the peaceful haven, then follow the stream into the wider world.

You travel beside the stream. It changes along course, perhaps deepening and widening, altering momentum, taking on a different colour and perhaps carrying flotsam with it. Perhaps you notice bottom of the stream or things at its side. Does it meander or run straight? Perhaps there are little waterfalls. Maybe the stream disappears below ground for a while, but you are still able to follow the path of its course on the land above. Maybe you can hear it still if you put your ear to the ground. As you travel, you observe the changes.

After some time, you reach the point where the stream enters a river. The waters mingle and take on a new appearance.

You realise you will need to find someone to ferry you if you are to travel along the river. You look around and see someone who can help. Approach them and talk to them to gain passage aboard a boat.

You thank the person who helped you, and climb aboard the boat, taking your place as crew or a passenger. You watch as the boat's captain readies it to depart and casts off from the shore. Slowly the boat sets off, and the gap of water between it and the bank widens. The boat is manoeuvred into its course to travel downriver.

Once the boat is underway, you watch the changing river and the changing scenery along the bank. Perhaps there is countryside or buildings. If there are buildings, are these homes, waterside inns, or places of industry? Are there bridges or places to land or dock? Does the scenery change as you go? Maybe you spot wildlife or maybe there are people. What are they doing? Do they notice you?

You pass other boats, and other river passengers. Perhaps some of them acknowledge you or perhaps some of them sail past or are left behind without looking in your direction.

What is this changing scene telling you?

Then, peer down into the river to see what you find there, and what that also tells you.

After many miles the river broadens and becomes tidal. Sometimes you see beaches at its sides. You begin to hear the sounds of the sea not far off. The smell of salty water is in the air.

At last the boat reaches the mouth of the estuary and the boat is manoeuvred to dock. The captain tells you this is as far as they can take you. You disembark, but before you bid farewell, you exchange a few words with the captain that seem fitting.

Alone once more, you walk on to the beach at the edge of the sea. Soft waves are breaking on the shoreline.

You know that to fully complete your journey, you will have to venture into the sea, but before you do, leave behind things you cannot take with you. Divest yourself of anything you feel you cannot, or should not, take into the water. Leave them on the shore. Then, before stepping into the sea, spend a few moments watching and listening to the waves.

You move out into the salty water, the waves falling around your feet, but know you are safe and that this is the right thing for you to do.

At a safe pace, you move deeper and deeper into the water. It rises up your legs, above your thighs, over your hips. It reaches your waist and then your chest.

When you are ready, you know that you must make a decision. Will you plunge yourself entirely into the water so that it covers your head, or will you return to the beach?

Make that decision now. If you return to the beach, you do so safely and wait there watching the waves on the sea.

If you take the plunge, you submerge yourself in the ocean. You are completely within the element.

Suddenly, you feel the water swirling around. You know that you are safe and have plenty of oxygen in your lungs, but for a moment you are disorientated. The water has swept you up and you are being carried along by it.

You find yourself transported to a wonderful place, a place that is in a watery realm, but you know you are safe and that you can breathe easily here. Look around you. What do you see in this wonderful watery place?

You then realise are not alone, but are in the presence of a figure you know to be an elemental of water. You approach them greet them in the way that seems appropriate.

The elemental invites you to tell them of your feelings, hopes and fears that are in your heart.

They listen to what you have to say, and you feel they understand. Spend some time talking to the watery being.

The elemental then offers you a beautiful chalice and tells you to sip from it, then peer into its depths. You take the chalice and drink from it, tasting the water it contains and feeling it flowing into you, cleansing and healing and suffusing you with calm.

Peering into it, you see an image form in its depths. That image, you realise, shows you a message that is important to you emotionally. Spend a few moments contemplating this.

It is nearly time for you to go. You thank the elemental for their help and say you wish to return to your normal realm. The elemental smiles, and tells you that before you go, they will return to you the item that you offered at the spring, at the start of your journey. They thank you for it, but say you have earned its return. The elemental then gestures and the waters around you swirl about, moving you with them. When you are still again, you have returned to the shore. Any items you left on the beach are still safely there for you to reclaim.

Dress yourself and gather your possessions. Now it is time to return to normal reality.

When you are ready take a deep breath, shake your fingers and toes and open your eyes to the real world.

Chapter 5

Visualisations for Psychic Work and Creativity

Here are a few guided visualisations designed for helping with creative processes and psychic work including scrying.

The Magic Mirror in the Enchanted Tower

This visualisation was written for workshops I run on divination. It involves questing to find a magic mirror that can be used for scrying.

* * *

Find somewhere safe and comfortable. Sit and close your eyes. Take three deep breaths in and out and relax, then visualise the following:

Visualise that you are in a beautiful garden at the edge of a wood. It is a place where you feel safe. Golden afternoon sunlight falls on the flowers in the garden, the weather is pleasantly warm and gentle. Spend time picturing the garden, smelling the scents and listening to any sounds of the birds or the gentle rustling of leaves.

Now, you are going to leave the safety and sanctity of this delightful garden and venture to find the magic mirror in the enchanted tower. At the end of the garden is a hedge and in the hedge is a gate that leads into the wood. You know that in the centre of the wood stands an enchanted tower and in the tower is a magic mirror, but only those who are worthy and determined are able to find it. You have decided to try.

Leaving the safety of the garden you go through the gate and enter the wood.

A path winds through the trees and you follow it. Visualise

the path and the wood around you. Notice the sights, scents and sounds of the trees, the birds, the animals that live here and be aware of your own movement along the path. What is the path like? Is your going easy or hard? You persevere and continue.

As you progress, the shadows cast by the trees lengthen. You realise it is late afternoon and the sun has started to dip. You keep going along the darkening path. Be aware of the changes to the woodland around you and sky that you glimpse through the canopy of the trees.

It is dusk as the path leads to a clearing, in which there is a tower that reaches higher than the treetops, into the purpling sky.

You enter the clearing and approach the tower. There is a single doorway at its base. Stop before the door and examine it. What does it look like? How does it open?

You reach out and try opening the door... To your delight – perhaps with ease, or perhaps with difficulty – it opens at your touch.

Spiral stairs wind upwards inside the tower and you start to ascend. Around and around you go, higher and higher. Eventually, the stairs open up in a chamber at the very top of the tower. There are four windows around this chamber, looking out into the night sky in which the stars are clear and a full moon is rising.

The only thing in this room is a full-length mirror on a stand. Move towards the mirror, position yourself in front of it, and look into it. At first all you see is your own reflection and behind you the reflection of the walls of the chamber and a window through which shines the moon.

As you watch, the mirror fogs over, then clears again and instead of your reflection you see someone else. Someone wise and knowing. They are smiling.

'I am the guardian of the mirror,' they say. 'You have found your way here through the woods and found the door to the tower open. You have ascended the tower and made your way here. You are ready to learn the magic of the mirror. What is it that you want to see?'

Decide what you want the mirror to show you. Perhaps it is a place or a person, a scene from the past or from the future? Perhaps it is the answer to a question. Tell the guardian what it is that you want to see.

Again, the mirror fogs over, and when it clears again you begin to see something else. Allow time for the image or images to form, then watch as you see your vision granted. Continue observing as the vision unfolds.

After some time has passed, the mirror again fogs over, and then clears to show you the wise and knowing guardian of the mirror.

They say, 'What you have seen is all the mirror will show you this night. It is now time for you to leave. You may return again, at other times, to see other visions in the magic mirror, but now you must go.'

Again, the mirror fogs, then clears. You see your own reflection in the chamber at the top of the tower, but the night has ended. The sun is starting to rise through the window. It is dawn.

Leaving the room, you descend the spiral stairs and go out through the doorway at the bottom of the tower into the wood. You retrace your way along the path through the wood, back to the gate in the hedge and then into the beautiful and safe garden once more.

When you are ready, take a deep breath, shake your fingers and toes and open your eyes to the real world.

The Building of Ideas

Find somewhere safe and comfortable. Sit and close your eyes. Take three deep breaths in and out and relax, then visualise the following:

Visualise that you are sitting in a pleasant and familiar spot out of doors enjoying a few moments alone with your own thoughts before beginning your chores or work for the day.

Look around, enjoy the sights, sounds and scents of this place. You feel safe, comfortable and at ease. Spend a few moments taking this in.

As you are sitting and thinking, the germ of an idea comes into your head. It doesn't matter how fantastical the idea is, you know that you want to remember it.

What is that idea? It might just be the first thing that popped into your mind, it might be a word or two, it might be a sentence, it might be a picture or a symbol or a diagram.

Knowing that you need to jot the idea down before you forget it, you find a piece of paper and something to write with. Write or sketch something to remind yourself of your idea on the paper.

Just as you have finished writing or sketching, a sudden gust of wind pulls the paper from your fingers. It tumbles across the ground away from you.

You get up and go after it but, just as it seems within reach, another gust blows it further away. You continue to follow the piece of paper, but never quite seem to catch up with it.

At first you are led over familiar ground, but after a while you find yourself in an area you do not know.

You are certain that unless you recover your idea, you will not be able to remember it sufficiently to make use of it. So, you go onwards, following your idea down unfamiliar paths, even though at times your idea is almost out of sight. You hurry on through areas you have not seen before. Yet, however fast you go, you do not catch up with your piece of paper.

It blows around a corner and you follow again, but you realise you cannot see it. You fear it has vanished.

You look around – then you look ahead. What you see astounds you. You see a huge building like no other you have seen before. It is made up of thousands of different parts, of different styles. There are perhaps towers or turrets, walls straight or curved, crenulated or flat, flying buttresses, overhanging windows and every type of architectural style you can think of. It is made from all sorts of materials too. You might spot stone, wood, iron and steel, bricks and mortar, or strange materials you do not recognise.

All the parts seem to hold together, but in such a jumble it is hard to see where one bit ends and another begin.

Approaching the building, you are just in time to see a piece of paper spiral up into the air and fly in through a tiny upper window.

You feel sure it is your piece of paper and that it has got inside the strange building.

You approach the entrance to the building, but it is guarded.

Think carefully how you will persuade the guardian to let you enter, then approach them and gain permission to go through

Going past the guardian, you enter and find you are free to explore. You wander through courtyards and corridors, up spiralling stairs and sets of steps, along narrow corridors and long galleries. You look into huge halls, tiny rooms and bizarre chambers. Inside even more than out, the building is a patchwork of different pieces cobbled together, none complete in their own right and none of it totally stable. Here and there you see craftspeople patching up holes with bits and pieces that don't really seem to be of the same style, material or even function. All the time, you are searching for your lost idea.

After a while you climb a narrow staircase and open a small door onto a tiny room. Inside, someone is sticking a collage of paper to the walls. They have a tub of paste and a basket of scraps of all different thicknesses and colours. In their basket, you see your own piece of paper. The worker reaches to pick it out of the basket and daubs paste on their brush.

Quickly, you must do or say something to retrieve your paper before it is stuck on the wall and becomes part of the building forever – just one more lost idea.

Do or say that now.

You gain your paper. As soon as you have your paper in your hand, the entire castle shifts and changes around you. The walls and floor dissolve and then reshape themselves and instead of being in a small room, you find yourself inside the entrance of a massive hall with a high ceiling. It is full of light that streams through tall windows. The roof of the hall is so high that in the air above your head miniature clouds hover. In these clouds you see the images of all sorts of dreams, ambitions and ideas that people have had over the ages.

You also become aware that you are not alone. In the distance, on a dais at the far end of the hall, you see a figure you know to be the sovereign of this castle.

You approach them; giving them the greeting you feel is right.

'You have come a long way,' they say, 'but before I can give you my help, you must hand me your idea.'

You realise you must hand over the thing you have struggled so hard to retrieve.

The sovereign of the building of ideas takes the paper, tears it into tiny little pieces and then throws the pieces in the air. The confetti of paper swirls about and dissolves into mist. Then, the mist swirls – and reforming into a perfected image of your idea, but as yet still insubstantial. You spend a while staring at it, and realise that you know enough to make your idea whole in the real world, if you choose to. The sovereign of ideas then asks if you have any questions. If you do, spend some time talking with them before the conversation draws to a close. The sovereign of ideas then hands you a piece of paper. It is like the one you lost, but now it has more information on it. It is yours to keep and to work on further. They then tell you it is time to go. They clap their hands, and again the building around you dissolves.

When the land reforms, you realise you are back in your familiar place, where you were at the start of this journey. You also realise it is still early. The day is ahead if you. you have time to do your chores and also start to work towards realising your idea, if you want to.

When you are ready take a deep breath, shake your fingers and toes and open your eyes to the real world.

Gods and Goddesses in Creative Art

This guided visualisation is adapted from my earlier book *Pagan Portals – Poppets and Magical Dolls* and is intended to help you get inspiration for a creative magical work of art or literature.

* * *

Find somewhere safe and comfortable. Sit and close your eyes. Take three deep breaths in and out and relax, then visualise the following:

Visualise that you are in front of large and impressive wrought metal gates that stand at the entrance to a beautiful park. Look at the gate and visualise it as strongly as you can. Immediately in front of the gate, through the wrought metalwork, you can see a path leading to a lawn. In the distance, on the three sides of the lawn, are gardens of flowers, copses and groves of trees and a gentle meadow leading down to the edge of the water. Look through the gate and visualise the path and this beautiful parkland. Spend some time doing this.

When you are ready, visualise opening the gate.

Walk through, take the path and go across the lawn. You see that ahead of you the path splits into three – one route leading to the gardens of flowers, one to the copses and groves of trees, and one across the meadow down to the edge of the water. Decide which route you will take.

When you have picked your path, you start to walk again, along your chosen route. As you walk, you notice that at your chosen destination – the gardens, trees or water's edge – there are statues, shrines, pergolas and grottos. These become more obvious as you continue along the path and reach the part of the park you were heading towards.

After a while you reach your destination. Although the path continues into the gardens, trees and along the water's edge, you are free to explore as you will – stay on your path or leave it and wander through the gardens, groves or along the bank.

Look at what's around you, including the greenery and landscape. As you do, your eyes are drawn to the statues, shrines or other structures. You realise that the statues are of gods, goddesses, venerated beings, creatures and people from folklore and mythology – and also wise and respected ancestors and teachers. In the shrines there are icons and images, and in the pergolas, grottos and other small manmade structures there are all sorts of works of art, from sculptures to frescoes, depicting many different deities, archetypes and those worthy of respect.

Wander among them and look at them until you find one you are particularly drawn to. When you do find one that you are interested in, go up to it and study it. Walk around it and spend as long as you need studying your chosen work of art from all angles.

After a while, when you have studied the work of art, you feel inspired to draw, paint, sculpt, craft or create something that relates to it. Perhaps you want to sketch or paint it as it is, perhaps you want to mould a small version from clay, perhaps you feel an urge to carve wood or stone into something like it. Or, perhaps, you feel inspired to write a poem or other literary work. You hope to capture the essence of it in some way or to create something entirely new, but inspired by it.

Glancing to one side you notice that all the materials you need to create your own work have been set out for you. Use them as you will for your own creation, based on the masterpiece you have been studying. Take enough time to do this.

When you are finished, you realise it is time to leave the park. Put your materials and your project to one side, but know that you are taking the idea for the work you created with you.

When you are ready, return back the way you came. Retrace your steps, go along the path and cross the lawn to the gates. Know that even though you will leave the park and the creative project within it, you will take your inspiration for your own work with you when you leave. With that knowledge, open the gate again and walk through it out of the park.

When you are ready, take a deep breath, shake your fingers and toes and open your eyes to the real world.

* * *

You should use writing, drawing, painting or crafting materials to try to reproduce the work of art or literature you created in the visualisation. It doesn't have to be perfect – it could just be initial sketches. You can return to this as often as you like, perfecting your creation. You can also repeat the visualisation to get more inspiration. When your work is finished, you can use it as an item of veneration or meditation in your spiritual practice or keep it where it will inspire you in your daily life.

Chapter 6

How to Write Guided Visualisations

After being guided on visionary journeys, you might want to write your own. If so, here are some tips on how to go about it.

First come up with an idea of what you want to write a guided visualisation about. Decide its main focus. Let's start with an example: a guided visualisation to meet a goddess. You then need to consider whether you want it to be about that topic in general, or be more specific. In our example, perhaps it is a chance to meet a yet-unknown god or goddess in order to find a personal patron, or it could be intended as a way of learning more about a specific deity. Let's say we are going to write about a specific goddess – Aphrodite. There are a few things to do now:

- Research
- Brainstorm ideas
- Plan an outline

Research will help you find important facts and symbols relating to the topic of your focus. For example, symbols associated with Aphrodite include spring flowers and roses, apples and pomegranates, myrtle trees, doves, shells, mirrors, the metal copper, and a magical girdle that holds her power. She had many different forms in the ancient world. She was a nature goddess as well as being associated with love and sex. In some forms Aphrodite is male or intersex, and she is also the deity of Sapphic love. Sometimes she was depicted wearing armour and ready for battle, while she was considered terrifying because she could drive people mad with desire.

You need to brainstorm ideas to make your visualisation original. This means jotting down any thoughts that come into your mind that might be included. Some of these ideas will get used, others won't. It doesn't matter at this stage. My own initial ideas were that I wanted to include a garden, a beach and a temple in the visualisation, plus the saying that the road to true love never runs smooth.

Visualisations need a structure, which you should plan. Let's say, for our example, that the visualisation will take the form of a journey from a garden to Aphrodite's temple. On the way, various types of location and symbols can be encountered, while at her temple there could be statues of various forms of the goddess.

You can research, brainstorm and plan in any order. Some people are natural muses and come up with ideas easily and instinctively; others are better at doing careful research, whether that is reading books or looking things up online; some like to work out a structure first then fill in the gaps later. It doesn't really matter which is easiest for you, but you will need to do a little of all three things at some point or another. To help get more inspiration you could try doing the last two guided visualisations in this book.

Then, if you haven't done so already, open up your notebook or start up your computer and begin writing the visualisation. This means getting your research, brainstormed ideas and structure together into a cohesive whole. Things will change as you go along. Some of your ideas will be jettisoned, your structure might change, and you won't necessarily use all of your research. For example, when reading Bettany Hughes' book *Venus and Aphrodite*, I learned that in the ancient world one of the forms of the goddess was Aphrodite of the Beautiful Buttocks. While that might be historically accurate, if you say that in a guided visualisation everyone will giggle. Aphrodite also wasn't always nice. Some of her aspects are problematic in terms of 21st century ideas of sexual behaviour. You should think carefully about how – or whether – you want to include them; perhaps hinting by saying "Aphrodite of dark desires".

Creating a Guided Visualisation

Begin by ensuring those doing the visualisation are comfortably in a safe place where they are unlikely to be interrupted. You should then get them to relax and close their eyes, as that is likely to help them do the visualisation without being distracted. Then move on to the descriptions that will guide what they visualise.

It is best to start by asking them to mentally picture some sort of reasonably familiar place. It doesn't have to be a location they know – although it could be – but it needs to be the kind of place that is easy to imagine. Common examples are a room, a garden, a river or lake bank, or a beautiful place in the countryside.

You should write the script in the second person, using the word 'you' to describe what the visualiser does or sees. This is different from regular story writing, as most fiction is written in the third person – 'he/she/they' – or the first person – 'I'. You want the visualiser to feel as though they are experiencing things as immediately as possible. You want them to imagine they are seeing things with their own eyes, hearing with their own ears, and moving under their own volition.

The script needs to enable an experience of change happening. This often means taking them on a journey. They could go through a door or gate into another location, follow a path, go down or up steps, or take a boat, for example. However, the change might happen to the environment they are in. Perhaps it goes from daytime into night time, the lights brighten or go out, a mist appears and then clears. Maybe time speeds up and they notice the seasons change or they go back in time and the items around them reflect that. Be inventive, but make sure it fits in with the main theme and focus.

Often a guided visualisation will involve a meeting with a person, creature or entity. The visualiser might meet them along the route, they might enter the scene being pictured, or the meeting might be the climax of the visualisation.

The things that happen and are encountered should have symbolic importance relating to the focus you have chosen. For example, in our visualisation to meet the goddess Aphrodite, the journey could start in a garden with roses, spring flowers, myrtle and fruit trees. An initial task could be to choose a gift from the garden to present to Aphrodite at her temple.

Quite often a guided visualisation will include some obstacle or challenge that has to be overcome. This should be appropriate for the theme and focus. For example, Aphrodite is not always a gentle goddess. She can bring the suffering and anguish of love as well as passion and romance. This could be represented by a difficult, winding, rocky path between the garden and the beach. Another suggestion might be a hedge of thorny wild roses that has to be crossed. To emphasise that aspect, you could include a meeting with a someone who warns of these things.

The beach could present a chance for introducing more symbolism. Water is associated with the emotions, while the area between high tide and low tide is a liminal space where change is possible. Beaches are often scenes for romance, but in bad weather tragedy can happen.

After the journey or other changes, the visualiser should reach the most significant part of the visualisation. That might mean encountering the person or place that is the main focus. In the Aphrodite example, that might mean reaching a temple to the goddess, entering its inner sanctum and encountering the goddess herself. Perhaps she is there in person, perhaps there are statues of her representing her different aspects, or perhaps she can be seen in another way. You could perhaps ask the person doing the visualising to choose one of the statues to leave the gift they picked in the garden. Perhaps that statue then comes to life or communicates in another way. I mentioned that mirrors are associated with Aphrodite. You could say the visualiser sees a copper-bound mirror in the temple's inner sanctum in which they see the face of the goddess.

The script could encourage the visualiser to spend some time conversing with the person or being they meet, or otherwise encountering the situation. You could suggest they ask a question or look for an answer they are seeking, but do not be too precise in what you describe as happening at this point. The visualiser should be encouraged to experience what happens using images, words or feelings that come to them spontaneously. Their own subconscious and intuition should provide messages. Factor in a pause in the script to allow enough time for this to happen.

After this pivotal point, the script should indicate that the encounter or conversation is coming to an end. In our example you could suggest that the goddess gives her blessing or some words of advice and then disappears from view or changes back into a statue.

Then, the script should generally guide the visualiser back to the place in which they started the adventure. If they haven't gone on a journey, then the place they are in should return to the state in which it began. It is important to give a suitable and satisfying ending to the visualisation, and also to return them to a safe, relatively normal space and comfortable state.

Finally, make sure they fully return to everyday reality. This can be done by making them aware of the sensations in their real body – breathing, pressing their feet on the ground, shaking their fingers and wiggling their toes, then opening their eyes.

With any written work, you should always reread it and edit and improve it a few times after the first draft. When you are happy with it, try it out yourself to give it a test run before guiding others on the visualisation.

Final Words

I hope you have enjoyed the journeys we have been on together, and wish you many more adventures in the future. Life itself is a journey, but the symbols, messages and signs along the path can guide us safely past obstacles and help us find hidden treasures as we go. May you travel safely and in good company all the way.

**MOON
BOOKS**

PAGANISM & SHAMANISM

What is Paganism? A religion, a spirituality, an alternative belief system, nature worship? You can find support for all these definitions (and many more) in dictionaries, encyclopaedias, and text books of religion, but subscribe to any one and the truth will evade you. Above all Paganism is a creative pursuit, an encounter with reality, an exploration of meaning and an expression of the soul. Druids, Heathens, Wiccans and others, all contribute their insights and literary riches to the Pagan tradition. Moon Books invites you to begin or to deepen your own encounter, right here, right now.

If you have enjoyed this book, why not tell other readers by posting a review on your preferred book site.

Recent bestsellers from Moon Books are:

Journey to the Dark Goddess
How to Return to Your Soul
Jane Meredith
Discover the powerful secrets of the Dark Goddess and
transform your depression, grief and pain into healing
and integration.
Paperback: 978-1-84694-677-6 ebook: 978-1-78099-223-5

Shamanic Reiki
Expanded Ways of Working with Universal Life Force Energy
Llyn Roberts, Robert Levy
Shamanism and Reiki are each powerful ways of healing; together,
their power multiplies. *Shamanic Reiki* introduces techniques to
help healers and Reiki practitioners tap ancient healing wisdom.
Paperback: 978-1-84694-037-8 ebook: 978-1-84694-650-9

Pagan Portals – The Awen Alone
Walking the Path of the Solitary Druid
Joanna van der Hoeven
An introductory guide for the solitary Druid, *The Awen Alone* will
accompany you as you explore, and seek out your own place
within the natural world.
Paperback: 978-1-78279-547-6 ebook: 978-1-78279-546-9

A Kitchen Witch's World of Magical Herbs & Plants
Rachel Patterson
A journey into the magical world of herbs and plants, filled with
magical uses, folklore, history and practical magic. By popular
writer, blogger and kitchen witch, Tansy Firedragon.
Paperback: 978-1-78279-621-3 ebook: 978-1-78279-620-6

Medicine for the Soul
The Complete Book of Shamanic Healing
Ross Heaven
All you will ever need to know about shamanic healing and how to
become your own shaman...
Paperback: 978-1-78099-419-2 ebook: 978-1-78099-420-8

Shaman Pathways – The Druid Shaman
Exploring the Celtic Otherworld
Danu Forest
A practical guide to Celtic shamanism with exercises and
techniques as well as traditional lore for exploring the Celtic
Otherworld.
Paperback: 978-1-78099-615-8 ebook: 978-1-78099-616-5

Traditional Witchcraft for the Woods and Forests
A Witch's Guide to the Woodland with Guided Meditations and
Pathworking
Mélusine Draco
A Witch's guide to walking alone in the woods, with guided
meditations and pathworking.
Paperback: 978-1-84694-803-9 ebook: 978-1-84694-804-6

Wild Earth, Wild Soul
A Manual for an Ecstatic Culture
Bill Pfeiffer
Imagine a nature-based culture so alive and so connected,
spreading like wildfire. This book is the first flame...
Paperback: 978-1-78099-187-0 ebook: 978-1-78099-188-7

Naming the Goddess
Trevor Greenfield
Naming the Goddess is written by over eighty adherents and
scholars of Goddess and Goddess Spirituality.
Paperback: 978-1-78279-476-9 ebook: 978-1-78279-475-2

Shapeshifting into Higher Consciousness
Heal and Transform Yourself and Our World with Ancient
Shamanic and Modern Methods
Llyn Roberts
Ancient and modern methods that you can use every day to
transform yourself and make a positive difference in the world.
Paperback: 978-1-84694-843-5 ebook: 978-1-84694-844-2

Readers of ebooks can buy or view any of these bestsellers by
clicking on the live link in the title. Most titles are published in
paperback and as an ebook. Paperbacks are available in traditional
bookshops. Both print and ebook formats are available online.

Find more titles and sign up to our readers' newsletter at
http://www.johnhuntpublishing.com/paganism
Follow us on Facebook at https://www.facebook.com/MoonBooks
and Twitter at https://twitter.com/MoonBooksJHP

You may also like...

Pagan Portals – Candle Magic
A witch's guide to spells and rituals

978-1-78535-043-6 (paperback)
978-1-78535-044-3 (e-book)

...a 'must-have' introduction to the fascinating subject of candle magic
Mélusine Draco, author of the Traditional Witchcraft series of books

You may also like...

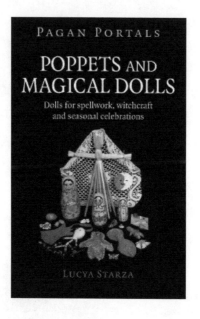

Pagan Portals – Poppets and Magical Dolls
Dolls for spellwork, witchcraft and seasonal celebrations

978-1-78535-721-3 (paperback)
978-1-78535-722-0 (e-book)

... concise but comprehensive, and both practical and inspiring
Joyce Froome, Museum of Witchcraft & Magic